MW01115515

S~~~~~~ ~~

BLOWOUT:

Corrupted Democracy, Rogue
State Russia, and the Richest,
Most Destructive Industry on
Earth

By
Rachel Maddow

CTPrint

CTPrint
Copyright (c) 2019

DISCLAIMER
This is a summary and meant to be a great companionship to the original book or to simply help you get the gist of the original book.

Table of Content

ABOUT THE ORIGINAL BOOK:

Blowout (2019) takes a deep dive into the murky waters of the global gas and oil industry and reveals just how toxic it is. Author Rachel Maddow looks at evidence of this in the US, along with the corrupt deals being made in Russia and Equatorial Guinea, and makes a strong case for why big gas and oil needs to be held accountable for its actions – before things get any worse.

ABOUT THE AUTHOR:

Rachel Maddow is a political commentator and host of the long-running and award-winning Rachel Maddow Show on MSNBC. She has a doctorate in political science from Oxford University and is also a best-selling writer whose work includes the book Drift: The Unmooring of American Military Power (2012).

Disclaimer: This book is not meant to replace the original book but to serve as a companion to it.

INTRODUCTION.

Discover just how toxic the oil and gas industry is.

You've probably heard about the Exxon Valdez spill of 1989, not to mention the Deepwater Horizon spill that devastated the Gulf of Mexico in 2010. But did you hear about the oil rig off the coast of Louisiana that toppled during Hurricane Ivan in 2004? As of 2018, it was continuing to leak seven hundred barrels of oil into the ocean every day, threatening to overtake Deepwater Horizon as the region's worst spill. It's still leaking today.

But the oil and gas industry isn't just harming the environment; it's also encouraging ongoing corruption and the imbalance of wealth and power around the world. This is especially the case in Russia, where that nation has put all of its chips on gas and oil being the country's primary sources of wealth and power. Despite these troubling problems, the industry continues to generate billions of dollars, and in chasing that money and new sources of gas and oil, it is earning its reputation as the world's most destructive industry.

In these blinks you'll learn:

How nuclear weapons were repurposed for the gas industry;
How much one corrupt politician spent on Michael Jackson memorabilia; and
Why Russian meddling in the 2016 election was more about oil than Hillary Clinton.

IN THE UNITED STATES, OIL EXTRACTION GOT GOING IN THE LATE 1800S, WITH JOHN D. ROCKEFELLER TURNING IT INTO AN INDUSTRY.

It all started on a Pennsylvania farm in 1859. Two men, Edwin Laurentine Drake and his hired assistant "Uncle Billy" Smith, managed to drill a hole and force a cast-iron pipe sixty-nine-and-a-half feet into the ground. What emerged was called "rock oil," and it led to an industry that has become one of the most dominant powers in the world.

That day, Drake and Smith got around twenty barrels of oil out of the ground. Fast forward to 2019, and more than 90 million barrels are being produced every single day. How did we get from there to here?

Well, the man who really turned the industry into the one we know today was John D. Rockefeller, the founder of Standard Oil and the guy who wrote the book on how to operate a ruthlessly successful oil business.

In his first twenty years of business, Rockefeller put the squeeze on and bought out any competitor that crossed his path. By 1875, he owned every major oil refinery in the United States. Other men were building up monopolies too, like those that Andrew Carnegie and Philip Armour created in, respectively, the steel and meat industries. None proved as lucrative as oil, though. Rockefeller was making so much money that paying off the politicians who regulated the industry amounted to just another business expense. Estimates suggest that, at his peak, Rockefeller was worth the equivalent of $305 billion in 2006 dollars.

In 1911, a landmark antitrust lawsuit led to the Supreme Court finding Rockefeller and his company guilty of creating a monopoly through unfair business practices. But the ruling only managed to divide Standard Oil into a bunch of smaller businesses, all of them still owned by Rockefeller. As a result, he was able to continue amassing his fortune and ended up richer than ever before.

Rockefeller also left the oil industry with a legacy of making sure no penny went unpinched. He kept a close count of every piece of inventory that was bought and made sure that nothing went unaccounted for or unused.

As the years went on, this focus on keeping operating costs as low as possible would continue to be the modus operandi of the oil industry.

WHEN US OIL SUPPLIES DRIED UP IN THE LATE 1960S, THE ENERGY INDUSTRY TURNED TO NATURAL GAS, WHICH IT TRIED TO EXTRACT THROUGH RATHER qUESTIONABLE MEANS.

Did you know that the US government gave nuclear bombs to oil companies in an effort to keep cheap energy flowing?

It happened in the late 1960s and early 1970s, when domestic oil supplies were dwindling and costs were on the rise. Concerned about keeping a steady supply of low-cost energy coming, oil companies started to look toward natural gas.

The process of extracting and capturing gas trapped under deep layers of solid rock requires the creation of fissures – fractures in the rock that allow the gas to seep out. This gave the process the name that it would come to be known by: fracking. According to the US Bureau of Mines, the Rocky Mountains held an estimated 317 trillion cubic feet of natural gas, enough to fuel the country for decades. The Austral Oil Company was already hard at work trying to tap the gas underneath land they owned in Rulison Field, Colorado, but their efforts had so far proved unsuccessful.

That's when the US Atomic Energy Commission, or AEC, stepped in: Since World War II the country had been building up a sizable collection of nuclear weapons, and a program known as Project Plowshare was exploring peaceful ways of using these atomic bombs. Why not team up with Austral Oil and use a nuke to loosen up all that precious gas? Surely it could be more efficient than cumbersome drills and derricks, right?

On September 10, 1969, Project Rulison commenced with a 40-kiloton nuclear bomb detonated 8,426 feet below ground, leaving behind a cavern 300 feet high and 152 feet wide. The good news was that the blast stimulated "the equivalent of approximately 10 years of production from a conventionally stimulated well in the Rulison field," according to the project's Manager's Report. But the bad news was that it left the gas "mildly radioactive," containing krypton-85 and tritium – and they couldn't be sure of exactly how much tritium, since they didn't have the proper device to measure it.

Over the next three years, two more tests with even more powerful bombs followed. But nuclear fracking never proved commercially viable. The bombs were messy, too costly, and not enough gas was being captured. In fact, throughout the 1970s, 1980s, and early 1990s, no one was able to come up with a commercially viable method to get at that deep underground gas. But then, in the late 1990s, a man named George Mitchell finally cracked that nut.

FRACKING BECAME ECONOMICAL IN THE LATE 1990S, THOUGH THERE HAVE BEEN HEALTH CONCERNS.

By the late 1990s, the oil and gas industry had more or less given up on fracking. Reaching the shale formations, that deep sedimentary rock that protected the natural gas, was easy enough. But fracturing it and keeping it open in order to let enough gas out was proving elusive. Many US oil and gas companies were instead focusing their efforts on securing foreign oil rights.

But then George Mitchell, founder of Mitchell Energy & Development Corp. – which eventually became part of Devon Energy – developed a kind of "fracking fluid," which would become known as slickwater. It was injected into fractures to keep them open, in a process that would become generally known as hydraulic fracking. It would revolutionize the industry.

The exact contents of the fracking fluid would become a highly protected trade secret. The possible disclosure of its ingredients, and whether those ingredients were spreading toxic fluids around farmlands and drinking water supplies, ended up being a hotly debated topic in federal courts.

The problem is, hydraulic fracking involves the high-pressure release of as much as 1.2 million gallons of slickwater at a time. Even if that fluid were safe to drink – and no one is claiming it is – a lot of it ends up reemerging from the ground after having mixed with subterranean elements that are often radioactive or poisonous. Frackers attempt to contain or dispose of this wastewater safely, but it's not uncommon for it to spill into the area surrounding a fracking site.

Nearby residents have seen their pets and livestock die, and the people themselves have suffered from symptoms of arsenic poisoning because toxic wastewater got into pastures, freshwater springs, and drinking wells. Tests have shown areas around fracking sites to contain chemicals such as ethanol, butanol and propanol – all known to be slickwater additives.

Of course, no one wants these deaths and illnesses to occur. Nobody wants the chemicals in fracking fluids to enter the bloodstream of a house pet or a human being. So the question becomes, what steps are being taken to ensure that this doesn't happen?

As we'll see in the next blink, while the oil and gas industry is great at getting things out of the ground, selling them around the world and making obscene amounts of money, it's not very good at cleaning up after itself.

THE OIL INDUSTRY IS NOTORIOUS FOR FAILING TO PREVENT ACCIDENTS AND FOR NOT CLEANING UP THE ENVIRONMENTAL MESSES IT HAS MADE.

Even if you're not a news junkie, you've probably heard about the Deepwater Horizon accident. In April 2010, a series of grievous mishaps on an offshore oil rig in the Gulf of Mexico led to 11 workers going missing and presumed dead and nearly 5 million barrels of oil being dumped into the sea. The disaster got the world's attention, but it's far from an isolated event.

Less than two weeks after the Deepwater Horizon catastrophe, an ExxonMobil pipeline off the coast of Nigeria released 25,000 barrels of oil into the Niger delta. But that isn't exactly unusual either, since a 2006 report showed that 546 million gallons of oil have leaked into that same delta over the past 50 years. That's an average of 11 million gallons of oil every year.

ExxonMobil is no stranger to spills, having caught the world's attention in 1989 when its tanker, the Valdez, ran ashore off the coast of Alaska, leaking nearly 11 million gallons of oil. So you might expect the company to have been well-prepared when the US government called on it to help BP with its Deepwater Horizon spill. Indeed, by this time the company had developed a 580-page plan on how to respond to spills.

But as it turned out, none of those pages contained an effective method for containing the mess. Efforts such as a containment dome didn't work, and neither did putting hundreds of thousands of gallons of chemical dispersants into the ocean. The oil industry wouldn't reveal the ingredients of the dispersants BP and ExxonMobil were using either, and aside from not helping matters, the substances made cleanup workers feel nauseous after prolonged exposure.

Frustration over the industry's inability to enact a useful emergency response plan was voiced by Congressman Ed Markey, who dressed down the heads of the industry in a congressional subcommittee meeting in June of 2010. Markey got ExxonMobil's CEO Rex Tillerson to admit that "We are not well-equipped to handle [major spills] . . . . That's why the emphasis is always on preventing these things from occurring."

Yet, as the investigation into Deepwater Horizon would prove, the accident was preventable. It was the result of bad cement having been used to seal the well, lackadaisical monitoring and control of pressure, and faulty backup systems. From top to bottom, the people involved were found to be guilty of cutting corners in efforts to save time and money.

OKLAHOMA OFFERS AN EXAMPLE OF THE EXPLOITATIVE AND MONEY-HUNGRY NATURE OF THE OIL AND GAS INDUSTRY.

There are many examples of just how much the oil industry values money over the safety and well-being of people, but one of the most vivid examples is in Oklahoma.

Oklahoma is just one of the states that has experienced a boom in fracking operations. Throughout the first decade of the 2000s, land across the country was getting bought up left and right in a mania for unlocking more natural gas. In fact, natural gas was being promoted by the industry as the great salvation: still cheap, and much cleaner and less of a threat to the environment than oil.

Some Oklahomans, like Chesapeake Energy's Aubrey McClendon and oil tycoon Harold Hamm, were making billions, and yet the state itself was entering an economic and public health crisis.

McClendon was at the forefront of the fracking boom and had amassed thirty million shares of Chesapeake stock, which was going for $70 a share in the summer of 2008. Meanwhile, between the years 2008 and 2013, the state revenue from taxes related to oil and gas production decreased from $1.14 billion to $529 million. During that time, teachers in Oklahoma would become the third-lowest- paid in the country, and many public school districts moved to four-day weeks simply because the state couldn't afford a full five. The state's infrastructure began to backslide badly, with new schools so poorly built that they couldn't protect kids from the tornadoes that routinely terrorized the state; seven children even died in a 2013 tornado.

Yet even in the face of protesting families and teachers, oil and gas industry lobbyists would continue to fight to keep the state's production tax rates down to 1 or 2 percent. Despite the fact that drilling was regularly happening in states with tax rates of 10 or 12 percent, industry leaders were warning that even a single percentage rise would chase business out of Oklahoma.

What's more, science was revealing that fracking caused earthquakes – some so strong that they exceeded 5.0 on the Richter scale. But despite the ongoing damage to homes in Oklahoma and growing concern among residents there, news that the earthquakes were anything but "natural" was being denied and even suppressed by the industry. The powerful Oklahoma oil tycoon Harold Hamm went so far as to tell a dean at the University of Oklahoma that he'd like to see the scientists investigating the earthquakes be dismissed.

THE EXXONMOBIL CORPORATION HAS A TROUBLING HISTORY OF LOOKING THE OTHER WAY WHEN IT DEALS WITH CORRUPT GOVERNMENTS.

Along with using its lobbying power to keep its tax rate as low as possible – even if that tax money is desperately needed – the oil industry has a tendency to do business with some rather shady political players around the world.

Take the corrupt government of Equatorial Guinea, for example. The country has one of the highest per capita incomes in the world, earning an average of $37,200 for every person; much of that money comes from deals with ExxonMobil. Yet 77 percent of the population in the country live in poverty, and between 1990 and 2007, when the amount of oil revenue went up from $2.1 million to $3.9 billion, the infant mortality rate managed to increase from 10 to 12 percent and clean water remained scarce for 57 percent of the population.

While all of that oil money doesn't seem to be making it to the people of Equatorial Guinea, it is certainly making it to the country's president for life, Teodoro Obiang Nguema Mbasogo, and his flamboyant, spend-happy son, Teodorin Nguema Obiang Mangue.

When Teodorin was earning a reported $60,000 a year as the country's minister of agriculture and forestry, he moved $75 million through US banks, buying up a luxury estate in Malibu and a $38.5 million private jet. Other spending sprees included dropping over $1,700 on two wine glasses, renting villas at $7,000 per night, and spending a total of $1,398,062 on Michael Jackson memorabilia.

There have been ongoing investigations into the government of President Obiang, who is ranked at number eight on a Forbes list of wealthiest world leaders. And some might wonder whether ExxonMobil's business relationship isn't supporting the terrible situation in the country. But the company has gone on the record saying that it's not interested in how money gets used once it's placed into the hands of someone like President Obiang.

As one ExxonMobil spokesman put it in 2005, "[I]t is not our role to tell governments how to spend their money." What's also on record is that Equatorial Guinea represents 10 percent of Exxon's global oil supply, and the nation has the region's most industry-friendly tax and profit-sharing policies, according to the International Monetary Fund. So it's not hard to understand why Exxon is in no hurry to rock the boat in its mutually beneficial relationship with President Obiang.

THE RUSSIAN GOVERNMENT HAS BEEN RUTHLESS IN CONTROLLING ITS OIL RESOURCES.

Perhaps even more troubling than ExxonMobil's dealings in Equatorial Guinea has been its relationship with another world leader who keeps complete control over his country's oil supply: Russia's Vladimir Putin.

The story of how Russia's oil supply came to rest under the thumb of the Kremlin is a long one. Suffice it to say that since the fall of the USSR, various entrepreneurs have tried to launch their own oil businesses. But the successful ones have ended up being forced to sell to companies owned and operated by the Kremlin.

Today, the biggest of those companies is Gazprom, which controls Russia's natural gas industry as well as some media and television businesses, and Rosneft, which essentially runs the nation's vast oil supplies. The problem is that these are not well-run organizations — entirely corrupt and employed by Putin as blunt tools of political force, both companies bleed money.

Studies suggest that Gazprom loses around $40 billion a year due to corruption and waste, and the US State Department has characterized the company as "inefficient, politically driven and corrupt." Or as James Grant, the founder of Grant's Interest Rate Observer, puts it, Gazprom is "the worst-managed company on the planet."

Nevertheless, Russia is a primary source of oil and natural gas in and around Europe, and Putin has been ruthless in taking advantage of this. Gazprom, in particular, has been a powerful tool in Russia's aggressive relations with Ukraine, especially once the latter nation began to eye the possibility of entering the European Union. In 2006, Russia shut off its gas supply to Ukraine, forcing Ukraine to siphon off a portion of the gas that was moving through its country from Russia to other places like Hungary, Austria, and Slovakia for its own use. Russia then pointed the finger at Ukraine and said that this response was a sign that Ukraine would make an unreliable partner in the European Union.

This was not only a power play against Ukraine, but also a ploy to drum up support for the new Nord Stream pipeline that had been built between the European Union and Russia, bypassing Ukraine altogether.

Since Russia has put all of its eggs in the oil and gas industry basket, this is really the only muscle it can flex. Without any homegrown competition, and with money steadily leaking out due to corruption, Russia's oil and gas industry has not invested properly in research and development for new technologies or alternative energies.

This also means that Putin needs outside help for any significant projects, like trying to drill in the Arctic. Fortunately for Putin, ExxonMobil CEO Rex Tillerson is happy to do business while asking few questions.

RUSSIA'S RELIANCE ON OIL RESOURCES FOR ITS STATUS AS A WORLD POWER HAS HAD FAR-REACHING CONSEqUENCES.

In 2013 and 2014, Rex Tillerson was trying to land an oil deal with Iraqi Kurds that would be worth billions of dollars. The deal would ensure that profits were sent straight to Kurdish-run banks and not to the central Iraqi government.

The Obama administration made direct pleas for ExxonMobil to step away from the deal, as it would undermine efforts being made to build a peaceful coalition among the nation's Sunni, Shia and Kurd populations. As a 2017 New Yorker article pointed out, creating an independent revenue source for the Kurds would only worsen the fractures within Iraq.

But Tillerson went ahead with the deal. After all, there was nothing explicitly illegal about it, so why should it be different from any other deal?

A similar scenario presented itself in the partnership between Tillerson and Putin, a relationship that resulted in Tillerson being awarded the Russian Federation's Order of Friendship in 2013.

Both men wanted to start drilling in the Arctic as soon as possible. In this case, Putin had the drilling rights and the best ice-breaking sea vessels in the world, while ExxonMobil had the drilling technology and know-how to get the job done. Complicating matters was the fact that Putin had been racking up sanctions in 2014 as a result of Russia's illegal annexation of Ukraine's Crimea, as well as the fact that the ongoing conflict resulted in a Malaysia Airlines jet being shot down over Ukraine, killing more than two hundred people.

So on September 12, 2014, the US government informed ExxonMobil that, due to sanctions against Russia, the company was now legally required to stop its joint operations with the state-controlled Russian oil company Rosneft. Ultimately, ExxonMobil was granted two weeks to pack its bags and shut things down safely. But of course ExxonMobil and Rosneft continued drilling, and on September 27, 2014, Rosneft announced they'd struck oil 7,000 feet below the Kara Sea – just squeaking in under the two-week window!

While Russia's dealings with Ukraine may have led to sanctions, they also led to subversive new online tactics. Back in 2013, the Internet Research Agency, based in St. Petersburg, Russia, began developing ways of using the internet and social media to spread seeds of disruption around the world.

Employees worked in shifts, 24 hours a day, to create fake social media accounts as part of online campaigns, such as supporting Ukraine's pro-Russian separatists and spreading lies about the pro-EU side of the conflict. And, perhaps most famously, supporting Donald Trump's 2016 US presidential bid.

Unsurprisingly, the Russian agents of the Internet Research Agency were also big supporters of Rex Tillerson getting appointed as US Secretary of State.

THE BIPARTISAN EFFORTS IN THE UNITED STATES TO KEEP RUSSIAN SANCTIONS IN PLACE IS A SIGN OF HOPE, BUT MORE STEPS NEED TO BE TAKEN:

Arguments have been made that Russian support for Donald Trump's campaign was due to Putin's great dislike of Hillary Clinton. But a more persuasive argument can be made to suggest that it was all about oil.

Russia needs international help in sustaining and expanding its oil industry, and the Ukraine sanctions have made getting that help extremely difficult. That's why Russian representatives met with the Trump campaign in that infamous June 2016 meeting at Trump Tower. The question was: Would Trump support lifting the sanctions if elected? After all, the pending deal to build a Trump Tower in Moscow was also stuck in limbo because of those troublesome sanctions.

As it turned out, one of President Trump's earliest acts in office was an attempt to get the sanctions lifted. Fortunately, the US government worked as intended and blocked those efforts. Once the Senate discovered the Trump administration's intentions, Republican Senator John McCain and Democratic Senator Ben Cardin orchestrated a lightning-fast response, pushing through legislation that codified the sanctions and made them far more difficult for Trump to get rid of.

Of course, both Trump and Secretary of State Tillerson complained and pushed back against the legislation, but sweeping approval – the vote was 98 to 2 in the Senate and 419 to 3 in the House – meant that Trump had no choice but to sign it.

This example of democracy in action can be seen as a beacon of hope, since it shows that it's possible to slow down an industry that, if left to its own devices, will continue to cause corruption and geopolitical imbalance and poison the planet. But more regulations need to be passed.

A good example of such a regulation that almost came to pass is US participation in the

Extractive Industries Transparency Initiative, or EITI, an international effort aimed at holding the oil and gas industry accountable for where its money comes from and goes to. US willingness to join the initiative followed a troubling bipartisan Senate report called "The Petroleum and Poverty Paradox: Assessing US and International Community Efforts to Fight the Resource Curse." But early in his presidency, Trump quickly pulled the United States out of the EITI, to the dismay of those who were hoping for more corporate responsibility.

There is an abundance of evidence to show how the oil and gas industry is playing a huge role in causing geopolitical and environmental destruction. It's time for this most lucrative of industries to begin to pay for what it's done.

FINAL SUMMARY:

The key message in these summary:

The oil and gas industry continues to harm the environment through its negligence regarding toxic oil spills. It also continues to encourage the geopolitical imbalance in the world through business deals with corrupt governments such as Russia and Equatorial Guinea. In the name of more money and greater supplies of gas and oil, the industry has continually acted in the interest of quick profits, no matter the collateral damage.

About CTPrint

CTPrint is dedicated to creating high-quality summaries of non-fiction books to help you through the bestseller list each week!

We cover books in self-help, business, personal development, science & technology, health & fitness, history, and memoir/biography. Our books are expertly written and professionally edited to provide top-notch content. We're here to help you decide which books to invest your time and money reading.

Absorb everything you need to know in 20 minutes or less!

We release new summaries each and every week, so join our mailing list to stay up-to-date and get free summaries right in your inbox!

Made in the USA
Columbia, SC
25 March 2020